FOUND
Hope for Every Prodigal

21-DAY DEVOTIONAL
Greta M. Brokaw

Copyright © 2023 by Greta M. Brokaw

All rights reserved.
ISBN: 9798396887046

Scripture Quotations taken from the
King James Version (KJV)
public domain

DEDICATION

To all the prodigals, near and far, there is hope for you.

No matter what anyone else has told you, God can soak your sordid story with grace. It's not too hard for Him. No sin is too great. You are not too far away. And He delights to take our broken pieces and restore them.

God loves You. He sees You. He is chasing You.
And He is faithful to forgive.

Take it from a reformed prodigal, no matter how lost you are, by God's grace, you can be FOUND.

To my dear sweet Dad, Gary Becker, who invested in more prodigals than I can count, including me.
I can't wait to see you again.

INTRODUCTION

Every prodigal has a story, and sadly for many, it started in church. And if you're like me, it may have even started under a pastor's roof. The truth is prodigals are everywhere. Some leave. Some quietly stay. But either way, they are often produced over time, and we never want to be part of that production line. Rather, we want to be in the restoration business, and we can be.

The dictionary definition of "prodigal" is one who is "extravagantly wasteful", and whether through wrong living or just wrong thinking, we all have moments where we extravagantly waste God's grace. We don't take it when we should. We don't give it when we should. And we can never praise Him enough for it.

We often refer to the Prodigal Son of Luke 15, and while there is much to learn from that parable of Jesus, the Bible is stuffed to the gills with actual, factual prodigal stories as well. Adam was the first prodigal (a sneaky, hiding-in-the-garden kind of prodigal, to which I can relate), and so we each have at least a little bit of prodigal in us. And I know I

INTRODUCTION

have plenty of prodigal in me, but by taking a long look at God's Word and a long look at ourselves, we can learn how to pray for the prodigals of today and prevent the prodigals of tomorrow.

With subject matter that hits close to home, I wish I could tell you that I dove into this writing venture with great gusto, but God would know I was lying. Like every worthwhile pursuit in my life, this study (a Bible study/self-study) has been red-letter stamped with God's patient grace, my reluctant obedience, and all the things I've learned the hard way.

I don't like to talk about it, but the simple fact is, I can talk about prodigals because I was one.
But God.
But grace.

Beyond comprehension, the Sovereign Lord of the universe delights to redeem and restore prodigals like me. He can turn a Proverbs 5 girl into a Proverbs 31 woman, and that message is worth humiliating myself a thousand times over.

And I'm not the only one. I married a restored prodigal. I'm related to restored prodigals. I meet weekly with one group and bi-weekly with another group of girls who have been gripped by grace – all different prodigal stories, but all punctuated with a loving, forgiving Heavenly Father at the end of the road. So I know there's hope. And whether you are the prodigal or the prayer warrior in your story, I want to give you that hope, and I want to point you over and over again to the power of the cross.

I say some hard things in this book, but please know that I say them with love and a genuine desire to make your prodigal road smoother than mine.

INTRODUCTION

I remember a Sunday School teacher I knew helping a class full of little ones to memorize the 23rd Psalm. Because several of the children were too young to read, she used a series of pictures to prompt them for each verse. For verse 6, she held up a drawing of three little lambs, which she named **Shirley, Goodness, and Mercy**, and of course, she told her students that these sweet, smiling lambs loved to follow people around.

Now well into my fifties, I can gratefully say that **Shirley, Goodness, and Mercy** are still nipping at my heels. They have trailed behind me into places I didn't belong, places they should have never had to see. But thanks to His goodness and mercy, this prodigal girl has been undeservedly but undeniably **FOUND**.

And praise God, I wasn't the first, and I won't be the last.

By God's grace, prodigals still come home every day.
Never let go of that hope.

Praying for you and yours,

Greta Brokaw

P.S. – I've included lists at the back for you to track your Prayer Requests, Answered Prayers, and other notes on this journey. Let's be amazed by God's goodness and mercy.

ARE YOU SAVED?

As you pray for God to change your prodigal, be sure that you've made the most important change for yourself:

1. **Life is short.**
   "For what is your life? It is even a vapour, that appeareth for a little time, and then vanisheth away." – James 4:14b

2. **Death is sure.**
   "And as it is appointed unto men once to die, but after this the judgment." – Hebrews 9:27

3. **Sin the Cause.**
   "For all have sinned, and come short of the glory of God." – Romans 3:23

4. **Christ the cure.**
   "But God commendeth his love toward us, in that, while we were yet sinners, Christ died for us." – Romans 5:8

   "For the wages of sin is death; but the gift of God is eternal life through Jesus Christ our Lord." – Romans 6:23

   "For whosoever shall call upon the name of the Lord shall be saved." – Romans 10:13

Pray a simple prayer.

It doesn't have to be fancy. Just tell the Lord that you know that you are a sinner and you cannot save yourself. Ask him to forgive your sins and to be your personal Savior.

That's all it takes.

If you prayed that prayer sincerely, you are forever saved (I John 5:11-13). But don't stop there! Get into the Word, get into a Bible-believing church, and get serving! God bless you.

TABLE OF CONTENTS

DAY 1	God's Lost & Found	1
DAY 2	Closest To Hell	4
DAY 3	Restoration Celebration	7
DAY 4	Ask Away	10
DAY 5	Users & Abusers	14
DAY 6	The Bottom of The Barrel	17
DAY 7	Unconditional Grace	20
DAY 8	Labels Lifted	23
DAY 9	The Dutiful Vs. The Faithful	26
DAY 10	Sin In the Camp	30
DAY 11	The Ugly Exit	34
DAY 12	It Is Enough	38
DAY 13	Restore Such a One	41
DAY 14	Peter the Prodigal	45
DAY 15	Home Sweet Home	49
DAY 16	Restoration Business	54
DAY 17	Betting with Barnabas	57
DAY 18	Deep-End Disasters	60
DAY 19	People in the Path	64
DAY 20	For a Season	67
DAY 21	Pray On, Prayer Warrior	71

DAY 1

GOD'S LOST & FOUND

"Then drew near unto him all the publicans and sinners for to hear him. And the Pharisees and scribes murmured, saying, This man receiveth sinners, and eateth with them." – Luke 15:1-2

Scripture Reading: Luke 15:1-7

All too often, God's people are not on board with God's program. And while Luke 15 shows us God's undivided heart for the lost, the first two verses highlight the great divide in Jesus' audience.

The ones in the front row are the tax collectors and sinners, the obvious outcasts who know that they are despised by the temple, and rightly so. These people hold no illusions about their place in society or their relationship to God. They know they are in dire spiritual need, and Jesus offers them a hope of restoration that has never been within their reach before (Mark 2:16-17).

On the fringes, sitting in the seats of the scornful, are the scribes and Pharisees. Mortally offended by the attention and validation that Jesus gives to their wayward counterparts, they have come to counter Jesus' message of amazing grace with the original brand of Pharisaical judgment.

And here's the spectacular truth. Obsessed with the unworthiness of the people in the front row, the Pharisees don't realize that they, the ones in the flowing robes with the phylacteries (a small leather box containing written scriptures fastened to their foreheads), are the real prodigals. They're the ones who have taken their God-given inheritance, extravagantly wasted it, and run away in the wrong direction. They're the ones who are on the banks of the river of redemption but refuse to step into the living water (Matthew 5:20, 16:1-4, 22:15, 23:27, Mark 12:12, Luke 11:53-54, 20:20-26, John 4:14, 8:3-11).

They think that their righteousness is sealed by the blood of their fathers, their proximity to the temple, and the pious performance of a thousand rituals. There's a long-running joke in Baptist circles that the backslidden sit in the back row of the church, but on this day, it was actually true.

The same mindset plagues many modern-day prodigals, particularly pastor's kids and ministry kids, and I have this exhortation to offer (because I learned it the hard way). Never mistake proximity for personal relationship. It's one thing to sit in a pew every week; it's another to sit in the presence of a Holy God (Matthew 7:22-24, 15:8). One is checking a box; the other is checking yourself (before you inevitably wreck yourself).

For years, I lived in the back row of these verses, smug and comfortable and convinced that I could do no wrong - that I belonged because my dad was the pastor and church was my second home (Romans 3:10, 3:23, I Corinthians 10:12, Ephesians 2:8-9). How wrong I was. Older, wiser, and with a lot more wear and tear on my pride and my heart, I now understand that church as a second home doesn't guarantee a heavenly home. And while it's still wise to be at church every time the doors are open, perfect attendance is no substitute for real repentance.

Whether a prodigal is inside or outside of the church, pray that they find their way to the front row and their own ongoing personal relationship with Jesus (Romans 12:1-2, Ephesians 3:17-19, Philippians 3:7-10). Pray that they are not only saved but sanctified. Pray that they are in the Word, and not just in church. And pray that, deep in the recesses of their heart, they are truly with God's program.

PRODIGAL PRAYER

Lord, help _____ to earnestly desire a personal relationship with you. No family status or ministry position and no proximity to the church replaces a real and right personal relationship with you.

Please reveal any wrong ideas about who You came to seek and to save, and please give us humble hearts that long to be closer to You, to know Your Word and live it, and to rely only on You for salvation.

DAY 2

CLOSEST TO HELL

"And he spake this parable unto them, saying, What man of you, having an hundred sheep, if he lose one of them, doth not leave the ninety and nine in the wilderness, and go after that which is lost, until he find it?"
– Luke 15:3-4

Scripture Reading: Luke 15:1-7, I Timothy 2:1-6

I remember my father praying, "Lord, save the sinner that's closest to hell." It sounds terribly morbid, but to die without a Savior is as morbid as you can get. And the simple truth is this – Jesus is the only Hope that puts hell in its place.

In this passage in Luke 15, I think it's imperative to note that all of the sheep are in the wilderness. All are in need of a Shepherd and a Savior, and yet the heart of Christ is to run headlong after the one that is closest to hell.

Verse 4 of tells us that the Shepherd leaves 99 sheep "in the wilderness" to go after the one in greatest danger.

That's an amazing detail. The other 99 aren't locked up safely in the fold. They aren't even necessarily lying down in green pastures by still waters, and yet, the Shepherd seems to prioritize the prodigal.

What a comfort. What a gift. When a prodigal turns ugly, turns their back on grace, and runs headlong into the worst dangers the world has to offer, Jesus starts running, too. It's almost as if He enjoys the challenge of loving the unlovely, saving the stubborn, and redeeming reprobate hearts. He pinned down Paul on the Damascus Road (Acts 9), and He can pinpoint your prodigal wherever sin has taken them (Job 34:21, Psalm 139:7-10, Hebrews 4:13).

Now don't get me wrong, as the self-appointed prayer warrior for a gaggle of various prodigals, it's terrifying when they truly go off the rails. But when they hit the wall, Jesus is sitting beside it, waiting to scoop them up. When they're down to surviving on corn husks in the pig pen of life, Jesus is standing at the gate, waiting to walk them home (Ezekiel 34:11-30, Luke 15:15-17, John 10:11-14). And when they've wandered so far into the wilderness that everyone else has written them off, Jesus is running in their direction, ready to forgive and mighty to save (Zephaniah 3:17, I John 1:9).

We question God's will all the time, but one thing is always His will – for "all men to be saved and to come to a knowledge of the truth." You can bank on that any day of the week (John 3:16, I Timothy 2:4).

Pray on, Prayer Warrior. Pray and fast and hold on to Jesus for dear life (Isaiah 43:1-2, 45:2-3, Matthew 19:26, Mark 9:17-29).

I know it's scary business, but the closer they get to hell, the harder the Shepherd chases them.

Never doubt it.

PRODIGAL PRAYER

Lord, if I'm honest, it is terrifying to watch _____ moving further and further away from you. I fear for their safety. I fear for their future. I fear for the consequences that they'll face, both in this life and in eternity.

Please protect them, but more than that, please bring them back to you.

Lord, I believe YOU are chasing them. I believe YOU are greater, and I believe YOU are working in this situation right now. Lord, I believe. Help my unbelief. In Jesus' Name.

DAY 3

RESTORATION CELEBRATION

"And when he hath found it, he layeth it on his shoulders, rejoicing. And when he cometh home, he calleth together his friends and neighbours, saying unto them, Rejoice with me; for I have found my sheep which was lost. I say unto you, that likewise joy shall be in heaven over one sinner that repenteth, more than over ninety and nine just persons, which need no repentance."
– Luke 15:5-7

Scripture Reading: Psalm 86

Jesus is all about the underdog. He's not interested in the self-reliant, the self-sufficient, or even the self-confident. It's not that He doesn't want to save them. He absolutely does. It's just that they have more to learn about themselves and Him before they become save-able (Matthew 23:12, Romans 12:3, Galatians 2:16, James 4:10, Titus 3:5).

But here's the fantastic truth. Once a lost soul allows itself to be found, heaven erupts. When a stubborn-but-weary wanderer finally gives in to the chase of grace, the angels applaud. And just imagine the party – the preachers and prophets and prayer warriors who have gone before, clapping each other on the back and shouting for joy over the restoration of your loved one.

It's not impossible. It's not out of reach. God is Who He Says He Is. This is the meat of John 3:16 and the heart of God – restoration and celebration (Jeremiah 32:40-42, Daniel 4:34-36, Joel 2:13-14, Revelation 7:13-17, 19:8-9, 21:3-5).

Hold on to that thought when they tell you they're done with God, when they tell you that the saints are just a bunch of hypocrites, and church is just a waste of time. Those are the enemy's lies, and they may run deep, but God's love is deeper still. The Shepherd is still chasing, just waiting for this prodigal to run out of road. He has not given up on them, and neither should you.

Pray for the day that they collapse in exhaustion (rebellion is utterly exhausting), and the Shepherd picks them up and heads for home. And picture the moment that you and yours get the news that the lost lamb was found.

Picture this, and it will inflate your faith just a little more (Psalm 27:13-14, Proverbs 13:12, Hebrews 11). God loves dreamers. He loves believers who actually believe in what they can't yet see. Hold on to this picture on the hard days, when you look down the road and no one's coming home yet, and no one came the day before that or the day before that.

Pray on, and by God's grace, one of these days you just might look down the road to see a Shepherd with a dirty, bedraggled lamb slumped on His shoulders. And just think – what a day that will be.

PRODIGAL PRAYER

Jesus, I long for the day that You bring my prodigal home. I know that nothing is impossible for You. I know that Your love is deeper than any pit that they could fall into, and I know You can meet them where they are right now. I thank You for Your compassion. I thank You for Your longsuffering love. I thank You for Your patience with me. I am not worthy.

Please cut through the enemy's lies. Please get a hold of their heart. Please bring them to the day when we can all rejoice at their return.

You are the Good Shepherd. Please bring Your lost lambs back home. I know that You can, and I believe it is Your will. In Your Precious Name, Amen.

DAY 4

ASK AWAY

"Ask, and it shall be given you; seek, and ye shall find; knock, and it shall be opened unto you: For every one that asketh receiveth; and he that seeketh findeth; and to him that knocketh it shall be opened."
– Matthew 7:7-8

"As many as I love, I rebuke and chasten: be zealous therefore, and repent. Behold, I stand at the door, and knock: if any man hear my voice, and open the door, I will come in to him, and will sup with him, and he with me.
To him that overcometh will I grant to sit with me in my throne, even as I also overcame, and am set down with my Father in his throne. He that hath an ear, let him hear what the Spirit saith unto the churches."
– Revelation 3:19-22

Scripture Reading: Matthew 7:1-11, Luke 18:1-8

I've never been diagnosed, but I am absolutely convinced that I have Attention Deficit Disorder when it comes to spiritual things. I can be praying circles around a problem or a prodigal one day, and not long after, I can completely forget to keep praying. My ever-reactive heart focuses on something else and yesterday's unanswered prayer request fails to make tomorrow's prayer list.

But there is a holy, prayer persistence stressed throughout scripture, particularly where prodigals are concerned.

In Luke 18, Jesus tells a parable about a persistent widow and a pragmatic judge. There's no mistaking the point, as the first verse tells us that Jesus told this parable so we would know to pray always and "not to faint."

The parable widow is relentless in her pursuit of justice, to the point that the otherwise-uninterested judge grants her request – simply to get rid of her. The woman leaves no doubt that she will never stop asking until she receives, and her persistence pays off.

If we're honest, most of us give up way too easily – even on the prodigals that we love so dearly. Fainting is a way of life for us. We pray for a day or two, maybe a few weeks if the situation is desperate, and then we simply move on in discouragement and defeat (I Chronicles 16:11, Psalm 42, Romans 12:12, I Thessalonians 5:17, I Timothy 2:8, Philippians 4:6-7). On some level, we believe the enemy's lies that the situation is hopeless, and we stop begging for the life-changing hand of God to move.

And I have to wonder, how many prodigals have we left behind because we merely passed through the garden of prayer, rather than tending it and cultivating it? How many times have we fallen just short of praying a prodigal home?

My friend, prodigals need persistence. They need us to persist in prayer, to persist in pursuing them, and to persist in loving them (Proverbs 24:16, Matthew 18:21-23, I Corinthians 13:4-8, Philippians 1:6).

In Revelation 3, Jesus is addressing the churches. After revealing the things He wants to change and challenging each of them, He states, "I stand at the door and knock." The previous verse tells us that God chastens those He loves, and then He starts knocking. The chastening is not a pushing away, but a pulling in. Chastening is God's way of chasing. Your prodigal's departure is not meant to be a forever leaving. It is meant to be an eye-opening, heart-softening, pride-breaking, soul-searching experience.

God's knocking on the door of your prodigal's heart is persistent and consistent – a gentle but ever-present knocking that's meant to turn a one-way ticket to destruction into a round-trip flight home.

And God calls you to be persistent and consistent as well. Truly pray without ceasing. Keep asking, seeking, and knocking on the door of heaven's throne room. Keep reaching out to your prodigal in loving ways, making the most of every opportunity to invite them home – physically and spiritually (Galatians 6:1-10).

Don't give up on your prodigal because God hasn't. And this prodigal journey is meant to be an eye-opening, heart-softening, pride-breaking, soul-searching experience for you, too. God is knocking on the door of your heart, inviting you to build your spiritual strength, exercise your deepest prayer muscles, and join Him on a miracle-working mission. He's inviting you to embark on a prayer path that runs parallel to your prodigal's winding road.

And by God's grace, both of those roads lead home.

PRODIGAL PRAYER

Father, I am so easily distracted. My prayers are not nearly persistent enough. Lord, increase my faith. Strengthen my prayer life. I want to keep asking, seeking, and knocking. I want to see you move in my prodigal's life. I want you to move in me. Change my prodigal, Lord, but change me, too. Give me a heart to pray for the lost and hurting and prompt me to reach out to them at every possible opportunity. Lord, please teach me to pray, and teach me to love. Thank you for loving me. Help me to remember how You found me when I was a lost and dying mess. Help me to relentlessly pray for my prodigal to be found as well.

Please, Father, please bring them home. I know You are able, and I will not stop asking. In Jesus' Name, Amen.

DAY 5

USERS & ABUSERS

"And he said, A certain man had two sons: And the younger of them said to his father, Father, give me the portion of goods that falleth to me. And he divided unto them his living. And not many days after the younger son gathered all together, and took his journey into a far country, and there wasted his substance with riotous living."
– Luke 15:11-13

Scripture Reading: Proverbs 1:1-23

Few verses leave a bad taste in my mouth the way that Luke 15:12 does. The prodigal starts his wayward journey with two very telling words, "Give me…"

It is the ultimate example of grace spent without gratitude, and sadly, even the most devoted of saints can approach God with a "Give me" attitude.

Like the son in the story, many prodigals are users and abusers. They take without a thought, spend without conscience, and repeatedly waste the grace given to them.

But more than that, they attract other users and abusers who slowly strip them of all the things they took for granted.

I remember a Sunday School lesson from my childhood on the "Prodigal Son" of Luke 15. The teacher told it with large, beautifully illustrated pictures. One image showed the son surrounded by a sordid array of laughing, drinking people – fair-weathered friends who partied until the son couldn't pay for the party anymore.

The next image showed him utterly alone, bent low, head down, no money left, and no users and abusers in sight (Proverbs 1:10-19, 32, 11:29, 13:20, 14:6). They had drained him, just as he had drained his father, and they had moved on to their next victim.

Can I tell you – the second picture is better than the first. Don't pray for your prodigal's happiness more than you pray for their repentance. I know it's hard but pray for the empty end of themselves that sends the users and abusers packing and leads your prodigal back home (Psalm 1, 73:1-22, 119:71, Jeremiah 30:14, Zephaniah 3:20).

The world's brand of happiness may seem like a good thing, but note what you're up against. The enemy is forever trying to convince prodigals that there is success and satisfaction to be found outside of a relationship with God. And the party people of the world are Satan's sales force.

We don't want our prodigals to settle into the false peace that the world gives. That false peace will spend away their youth and waste what may be their greatest potential for God, and that's exactly what the enemy wants. Of course, God will forgive and restore and use them when they repent, but how many opportunities will be lost in the meantime? How many more souls will be lured down the prodigal road by the fleeting success of your prodigal?

Pray that God opens your prodigal's eyes to the users and abusers in their life. Pray that they see their own ingratitude and their own sad end reflected in the people who are using them the way that they have used you. Pray that they have no peace outside of Jesus (II Chronicles 15:3-7).

Pray for grace and mercy, but pray for clarity, and pray that the petrified pride of "Give me" changes to the heartfelt humility of "Help me."

That's when heaven starts planning a party of its own.

PRODIGAL PRAYER

Father, this is a hard prayer to pray, but I trust that You know what is best. Please reveal the users and abusers in my prodigal's life. Even if it destroys their happiness and leaves them hurting, I trust that they will never have true joy and peace until they get right with YOU. Please take away any false peace that is preventing them from repentance. And help me to forgive the ways that others have used and abused me, knowing that I, too, have been forgiven much.

Thank you for your longsuffering love to those who ungratefully spend your grace. Bring us all into right relationship with you and a better understanding of just how abundantly blessed we are in Christ Jesus.

In Your Precious Name I pray.

DAY 6

THE BOTTOM OF THE BARREL

"And when he had spent all, there arose a mighty famine in that land; and he began to be in want. And he went and joined himself to a citizen of that country; and he sent him into his fields to feed swine. And he would fain have filled his belly with the husks that the swine did eat: and no man gave unto him. And when he came to himself, he said, How many hired servants of my father's have bread enough and to spare, and I perish with hunger!"
– Luke 15:14-17

Scripture Reading: Psalm 101

Nobody wants to see their prodigal hit rock bottom. As a former prodigal who is constantly praying for current prodigals, I know that there are gut-wrenching moments on the rebel's road home.

But here's the hard truth. Just because we're praying against the rebellion doesn't mean that we haven't contributed to it.

What makes this moment so impactful in the prodigal's life

is the complete absence of everyone – including his father. He is experiencing the lowest point in his young life, and no one swoops in to save him. And the fact that no one comes to his aid allows him to come to his senses.

I'm striving here for a balance between grace and truth, because Jesus embodied both equally, and both matter to God in everything we do.

So here it is. Too many of us chase our prodigals around with our checkbooks. Too many of us welcome their sin into our lives and our homes because we don't want to make them feel unwelcome. And too many of us allow our prodigals to drag us away from relationship with God in our pursuit of relationship with them (Deuteronomy 7:1-9, I Samuel 3:11-13, I Kings 11:3-4, Psalm 101:3, Proverbs 19:18, 29:15, Ecclesiastes 7:24-26, Romans 12:9, II Corinthians 6:14, I John 2:15-17).

One last hard truth, and then I'll let up for a while. Your prodigal has the potential to become an idol, and when that happens, you are contributing to both their rebellion and your own.

I am all for grace. No one needed and still needs grace more than me, but I know that, in my own sordid past, there were times when I desperately needed truth, and no one gave it to me. There were times when consequence might have gotten through to me quicker than compassion. There were times when being left "in want" might have caused me to want God (II Corinthians 7:9-10, Hebrews 12:11, Revelation 3:19).

I can't tell you where human grace turns into enablement. Only God knows that. I only know that, as humans, with imperfect love and only the slightest understanding of grace, we need God to direct us in the level and the kinds of support that we give to our prodigals. We need to be intentional about frequently having those conversations with Him.

Pray for clarity for yourself. Pray that God will show you when you are enabling. Trust that, when you finally stop trying to control the situation on your own, God is going to step in and do the work that only He can do. Most of all, don't pray for the deliverance of your prodigals, while paying for the prodigal party.

God understands your struggle. After all, He is a parent of prodigals. Like you, He sends rain on the just and the unjust and desperately longs for the lost to come home, but He wants them to be truly whole and completely reconciled to Him. And I suspect, dear reader, that in your heart of hearts, that is what you want for them, too.

Trust that God knows the way.

PRODIGAL PRAYER

Father, please show me Your way. My prodigal needs you, but I know that I need you, too. I also know that your purpose is to change me more and more into Your image. So show me. Show me where I am enabling. Show me where the balance between truth and grace lies.
  Forgive me if I have allowed my prodigal to become an idol. Forgive me if I have valued my relationship with them over my relationship with You. If I'm the one who needs to change before my prodigal can come home, please reveal that to me and forgive me. I never want to stand between You and another soul.
  Change my prodigal, but change me, too. Have your way in both of us. I surrender. In Jesus' Name. Amen.

DAY 7

UNCONDITIONAL GRACE

*"I will arise and go to my father, and will say unto him, Father, I have sinned against heaven, and before thee, And am no more worthy to be called thy son: make me as one of thy hired servants.
And he arose, and came to his father.
But when he was yet a great way off, his father saw him, and had compassion, and ran, and fell on his neck, and kissed him."*
– Luke 15:18-20

Scripture Reading: Ephesians 2:1-9

Now for the good stuff.

We pray and watch and wait, believing that there will come a day – a day when repentance is real and forgiveness can flow and grace can be poured without measure.

In Luke 15:18-20, we see permission from God to lavish our prodigals with love, total forgiveness, and full reinstatement, in the wake of total and sincere repentance.

To an extent, even this response takes faith, maybe even just as much as praying for their initial return. Note that there was no trial period, no probation, no "we'll see if he really changes."

In my experience, that's a hard pill for many to swallow, and I have even seen churches struggle with this. We want proof. We want assurances that we won't be fooled again, and in our flesh, we can tend to run more on offense than on mercy. Praise God, He gives second chances, third chances, and fourth chances, and wipes the slate clean each time. I wonder if our churches might redeem and retain more prodigals if we did the same (Exodus 33:19, Nehemiah 9:26-31, Psalm 119:164-165, Isaiah 54:7, Mark 9:36-37, Philemon 1:12-15).

In Luke 15, the father received the son with open arms and an open heart. The prodigal received his father's robe and ring, symbols of status within the family, and a celebration, honoring him as his father's son. It was everything he started with and more.

Some might have questioned the son's sincerity or his ability to reform, but not the father. He ran to meet the son with immediate acceptance and gave the benefit of the doubt because, in human interactions, that's what mercy really is.

You and I don't have the omniscience to definitively know who will fall again, leave again, or rebel again. We give forgiveness with humble self-awareness and with hope, because the truth is, we all live on that hope. Although some have spottier track records than others, we are all mortal and liable to fall.

And so, when a prodigal comes back, world-worn and heart-humbled, we offer a resounding "welcome home" and a whole lot of love. And we continue to bathe them in every bit as much faith-filled prayer as we did before (Isaiah 40:1-2, 35:3, 55:7, Luke 22:32, Romans 12:10, I John 4:18-5:2).

It's what we would want for ourselves. It's what Jesus gave time and again when He walked this earth, and it's why He went to the cross.

It's unconditional grace, and it really is good stuff.

PRODIGAL PRAYER

Father, thank You so much for Your unconditional forgiveness. Thank You that I don't have to earn it, because I know I could never deserve it. Please help me to give forgiveness to others the way You give it to me. Let me have faith that You can change even the hardest of hearts.

If boundaries do need to be put in place, may they be only the boundaries that please you and protect my prodigal. May those decisions be selfless and have nothing to do with my pride or my need for control. Empty me of myself and fill me with Your Holy Spirit for this delicate work.

Let me remember that I am as liable to fall as anyone. Let me lavish grace at the first sign of real repentance and help me to trust the rest to You. Help me to love and forgive like You. In Jesus' Name, Amen.

DAY 8

LABELS LIFTED

"And the son said unto him, Father, I have sinned against heaven, and in thy sight, and am no more worthy to be called thy son. But the father said to his servants, Bring forth the best robe, and put it on him; and put a ring on his hand, and shoes on his feet: And bring hither the fatted calf, and kill it; and let us eat, and be merry: For this my son was dead, and is alive again; he was lost, and is found. And they began to be merry."
– Luke 15:21-24

Scripture Reading: Luke 15:14-24

Let's talk some more about grace, because I can't get enough of it.

Every prodigal, every sinner in fact, wears the same label. It reads "Lost." But note the faith-filled declarations this father makes over his wayward son. He is no longer "Dead", but "Alive", and the label, "Lost", is replaced with the grateful, hope-soaked sentiment, "Found."

Let's talk about labels for a minute. Most labels are grace killers. They fly in the face of forgiveness and chip away at hope. Too many prodigals are forced to forever wear additional labels like "addict", "drunk", "thief", "adulterer", or even just "failure", "hopeless", or "loser".

But if we believe God's Word (and I believe we do), then repentance and forgiveness must be label-lifters. II Corinthians 5:17 tells us that, "If any man be in Christ, he is a new creature. Old things are passed away. Behold, all things are become new."

That precious promise is like an eraser on the rap sheet of every homeward-bound prodigal. What happens down the road is between that prodigal and God. What happens between that prodigal and the rest of us is a removal of labels and a fresh start (Psalm 56:13, 89:15-16, Ephesians 5:8, Colossians 2:6-10, Titus 3:1-3, I John 1:7).

True forgiveness can be wiser (Romans 12:3, I Corinthians 10:13, Romans 4:19, I Peter 5:8). It can lovingly and prayerfully set boundaries that should have been there in the first place, but it cannot hold the forgiven hostage with labels. It cannot beat them over the head with constant reminders of failure. What is under the blood stays under the blood.

In God's economy, yesterday's confessed sin does not follow us into tomorrow. It stays buried in the depths of the deepest sea, as far as the East is from the West, mercifully and gloriously remembered no more (Psalm 103:12, Isaiah 43:25, Micah 7:19, Hebrews 8:12).

And hope takes its place. Hope waits on the other side of forgiveness, as we are once again in right relationship with God and free to enjoy our shared inheritance with Christ.

Don't trade hope for the smug satisfaction of "I told you so." Don't limit tomorrow with the labels of yesterday. It won't be worth it when you realize that you're pushing away the one that God just pulled back.

When God brings your prodigal home, help them to forget what is behind and press on to what is ahead (Isaiah 43:1, Philippians 3:12-14). They do not need you to remind them of their track record. Satan will invest plenty of time in that. Give them hope. Give them the same pass that God gave you. Treat them like a new creature.

And remember, when a lost soul gets right with God, the only label worth keeping is the one that reads "**Found**."

PRODIGAL PRAYER

Lord, I thank you that every sin I have ever committed is under the blood. I praise you that I don't have to live in constant shame and defeat because Your grace is greater than my sin, and Your forgiveness is forever. Thank you for sending Jesus to die for me, because I know I needed a Savior.

Father, I need Your help to forgive others the way I have been forgiven. Prick my heart when I revert to the labels of the past. Help me to forget what is behind, and to not undo the work that You have done.

Help me to remember where I came from and to have the compassion and mercy for others that I so desperately need myself. Help me to trust that there is hope and a new creation on the other side of repentance and forgiveness.

Thank you for loving me just as I am, but thank you for not leaving me that way. In Jesus' Precious Name, Amen.

DAY 9

THE DUTIFUL VS. THE FAITHFUL

"Now his elder son was in the field: and as he came and drew nigh to the house, he heard musick and dancing. And he called one of the servants, and asked what these things meant. And he said unto him, Thy brother is come; and thy father hath killed the fatted calf, because he hath received him safe and sound. And he was angry, and would not go in: therefore came his father out, and intreated him. And he answering said to his father, Lo, these many years do I serve thee, neither transgressed I at any time thy commandment: and yet thou never gavest me a kid, that I might make merry with my friends: But as soon as this thy son was come, which hath devoured thy living with harlots, thou hast killed for him the fatted calf."
– Luke 15:25-30

Scripture Reading: James 1:19-27

When I hold this story up to my own life, I find I relate to both brothers, and that's not a good thing. Having spent my entire life in church (even my worst prodigal days), I now understand that this parable might be more-aptly titled, "The Prodigal Sons."

You see, only one son left the house, but these verses reveal that both sons had wandering hearts. And the "other brother", as I like to call him, shows a disturbing mixture of arrogance, heartlessness, and resentment that rivals his younger sibling's rebellion.

The other brother is dutiful, but not truly faithful. As soon as the father displays love and forgiveness, he is quick to stand on his own performance and deem his brother unworthy. He shares the father's home, but not his heart.

And oh, how many of us faithful (or should I say "dutiful") churchgoers are right there with him?

Take heed, dear reader. There is a brand of prodigal that never leaves the church pew, that shows up every time the doors are open, while secretly nursing resentment, a root of bitterness, and perhaps even a private prodigal life (Psalm 26:2, 44:21, Matthew 15:7-9, I Corinthians 10:12, Hebrews 3:12-13, 12:14-15).

And if they're like I was, they show up for their shift at church on Sunday, and stroll arm-in-arm with the world Monday through Saturday.

Worse still, these can often be the ones who are quickest to jump on the judgment bandwagon, as highlighting the failings of others conveniently shines the light in someone else's direction (Matthew 7:3-5).

Not only does this son lack compassion for his brother, but he is just as cold and unfeeling towards his father, refusing to allow his sweet dad even a moment of relief from the pain caused by the prodigal. And his unnerving mention of "harlots" (not referenced at any other point in the story), is a telling statement that betrays his own thought life, at the very least (Psalm 1, 101, Proverbs 4:23, 12:18, 15:28, 23:7).

I am ashamed to say that I spent about ten years living a prodigal life, fully engaging in the worst the world had to offer. Now, almost 20 years into my return, I still have to actively guard my prodigal heart. By God's grace, I have grown, but the process of renewing my mind and my motives never stops. And honestly, the worst temptations I fight are not the obvious "riotous living" appetites. Instead, I forever fight the temptation to cast the first stone, to forget where I came from, and to think more highly of myself than I ought to think.

As we pray for the prodigals who have visibly taken off down the road of rebellion, let us not forget that you don't have to go far to be far from the Lord (Deuteronomy 6, Psalm 139:23-24, Colossians 1:8-14). Every day, every minute, we need to examine our own prodigal hearts and ask ourselves, "Am I truly faithful to God, or am I just dutiful?"

Pray for the prodigals but pray just as hard for the good folks in the pews. Both are on the enemy's radar. Both run the risk of rebellion. And both can be less than faithful.

PRODIGAL PRAYER

Father, forgive us, we are needy people. Please bring back the prodigals who are far from home, and those who are far from You in their hearts.

Protect our churches. Work on the hearts in our pews and bring us all into right relationship with You. Help us to humble ourselves and pray and seek Your face and turn from our wicked ways.

Most of all, please show me the true condition of my own

heart. I know I can be easily fooled. Help me to be honest about the things in my day-to-day life that need to change. Let me see my sin as You see it, and as I wait for my prodigal to turn from their sin, may I turn from my own as well. Let me serve You with my whole heart. I want to be truly faithful to You. I want to hear You say, "Well done."

In Jesus' Name, Amen.

DAY 10

SIN IN THE CAMP

"Moreover if thy brother shall trespass against thee, go and tell him his fault between thee and him alone: if he shall hear thee, thou hast gained thy brother. But if he will not hear thee, then take with thee one or two more, that in the mouth of two or three witnesses every word may be established. And if he shall neglect to hear them, tell it unto the church: but if he neglect to hear the church, let him be unto thee as an heathen man and a publican."
– Matthew 18:15-17

Scripture Reading: I Corinthians 5

Hard things happen in the best of churches. And it should be that way. Every church, from the pastor's office to the farthest corner of the parking lot, is nothing more than a family of sinners saved by grace. But we serve a HOLY GOD, and therefore, sin can be forgiven, but never ignored. Sin in the camp spreads, and as painful as the process may be, when God reveals sin, the church needs to talk about it (Joshua 7, Ephesians 5:3, 25-27, I Thessalonians 3:12-13, I Timothy 5:20, I Peter 1:15, Titus 3:10-11).

I have been on the business end of this process. And I can tell you this: it hurts beyond belief, but it must happen. When a church is confronted with sin, they in turn must confront those involved. It is a simple matter of obedience to God's Word (Ecclesiastes 12:13, Ephesians 5:3, Hebrews 13:17, I John 3:10, Revelation 2-3).

We can talk all day about imperfect motives and poor execution and collateral damage (and in weak moments, I have). We can rage about hypocrites and "judge not", but it all comes down to this. In a fallen world, church discipline, as outlined in Matthew 18 and I Corinthians 5, is a necessary evil and a command from God. It breaks His heart as much as it does ours, but it is the truest form of tough love. And when done right, it sets the stage and sets a place at the table for restoration in time.

As a restored prodigal, I have suffered survivor's guilt for the things that, by God's sovereign and inexplicable mercy, never made the agenda at a deacon's meeting or required awkward conversations with pastors or public confession. I can't tell you why God allows one to be caught and others to fly under the radar, but in my experience, being caught is its own form of mercy. Disciplined or not, all prodigals pay a price, and often, the price for the unconfronted prodigal is more time in the wilderness and more collateral damage that might have been avoided by prayerful church intervention.

The Apostle Paul devotes much of his writing to problems, disputes, and sin in the church. I and II Corinthians alone are rife with the sin struggles of one congregation and exhortations to deal with it (I Corinthians 5:9-13, 6:9-10).

If you or someone you love has been on the business end of this process, my heart goes out to you, but I also believe there is hope for you. God blesses extreme obedience, and church discipline is just that. It may not be pretty, but God delights to give purpose to the "not pretty" things in our lives (Psalm 92:12-15, Isaiah 61:3-4, Jeremiah 29:11-13, Romans 8:28).

Don't let it make you bitter. Press into prayer. Your enemy will feed your discontent and rub salt in your wounded pride. But in God's design, this painful process is only meant to be fruitful.

One last caution. Beware of the church that would never go there, that values people's feelings and liberty and positive vibes over scriptural truth. They are on a dangerous road, and although they may be happily dancing down it, it is not one that God has told them to take.

Trust the process, not because you trust the people involved, but because you trust the God Who designed the process in the first place. Trust and obey, and God will take care of the rest.

PRODIGAL PRAYER

Lord, You know this is one of the hardest things for us to take. We want to pretend everything is all right. We don't want to risk losing anybody. We want to shield our prodigals and our churches from embarrassment, awkwardness, and open discussions about sin, but that only allows sin to spread.

Help us to remember that You are Holy. Help us not to hide sin, or excuse it, or look the other way, but Father, help us to confront sin in love. Most of all, help us to obey YOU, to do what You've told us to do, even when it hurts.

Help ME to trust the process that You have laid out and

to trust that You are working in that process, no matter what the immediate outcome may be. You are greater. You are good. And You are faithful to honor obedience to Your Word.

Thank You for intervening in the affairs of man to save souls. Thank You for Your loving guidance and Your perfect plan. Have Your way. I trust You, Lord. In Jesus' Name, Amen.

DAY 11

THE UGLY EXIT

"For I verily, as absent in body, but present in spirit, have judged already, as though I were present, concerning him that hath so done this deed, In the name of our Lord Jesus Christ, when ye are gathered together, and my spirit, with the power of our Lord Jesus Christ, To deliver such an one unto Satan for the destruction of the flesh, that the spirit may be saved in the day of the Lord Jesus."
– I Corinthians 5:3-5

Scripture Reading: I Peter 1:1-16

For many prodigals and their families, there is a moment - a horrifying, heartbreaking and even publicly humiliating moment - when life as they know it comes crashing down. In that moment, the church can feel like the enemy and God can seem a million miles away, like His glory has departed, and His back has turned.

I have personally been a part of moments like these, from all angles. They leave scars. It's the kind of devastating soul injury that will act up every time there's another storm on the horizon. Apart from the grace of God, you'll feel it forever.

And honestly, every time you set foot back in the church (assuming you do, because not everyone does), you'll hear whispers and feel stares that may or may not be there, and on some level, you'll question if you still belong.

I tell you all of this because your response is key. It will directly impact the trajectory of future generations. You are standing smack dab in the middle of one of the greatest gambles that the church is called to take, and God has given you the free will to determine whether His Church, His Bride, His House, and His People win or lose.

In I Corinthians 5, Paul confronts the Corinthian church on a not-so-secret sin situation. The entire church has turned a blind eye to blatant incest, and now Paul must personally supervise the ugly exit for the offending church member.

But although there is no doubt about what needs to be done, there is also no doubt as to what they are trying to accomplish. They will expel this man for a time, but with the hope that his expulsion will eventually lead to repentance and restoration (Psalm 51:7-8, Jeremiah 2:25, 3:22, Hosea 14:1-4, Isaiah 44:22-23, II Thessalonians 3:6, 14).

I cannot stress this enough. God has put a process in place, but as THE Master Planner, Great Creator, and Consummate Redeemer, every process of His is designed to yield a beautiful product. This is where we often fail to follow through. In our flesh, we can plow through the process, check off that box, and miss out on the product entirely.

Why? Because in God's economy, the recipe is always process plus prayer equals product, and we're talking LOTS of prayer – like at least 3 parts prayer to 1 part process.

Why are we willing to take the gamble of losing prodigals, losing whole families, and leaving the impression that some sins are unforgiveable? Don't we want to take that gamble, play it through and pray it through, and produce beautiful testimonies of mercy, forgiveness, and redemption that glorify God and draw other struggling souls to Him? If God tells me that I have to take that gamble with my family and my church, you bet I want God's glorious product and not just the hollow satisfaction of a process completed.

And to the hurting families, the ones closest to the ejected prodigals, I tell you with the ache of experience, HOLD ON. Hold on to the church (Psalm 84:10, 122:1, Hebrews 10:24-25). Hold on to Jesus (John 3:16-17, Romans 5:1-2, Hebrews 13:8). Hold on to hope (Jeremiah 17:7, Romans 5:3-5). Your response determines whether this will be a turning point or a spiritual breaking point for your family. Outsiders will tell you to leave in a huff. Insiders will often make you feel like you should. But God is working. It's not just a process to Him. It's the recipe for a specific and beautiful and eternally valuable product (Ecclesiastes 3:11).

But beautiful things take time.

Church, love on these families (Luke 10:36-37, II Corinthians 1:3-4, Ephesians 4:1-3). Go out of your way and make the first move. Don't leave them drifting in a sea of grief and embarrassment. The enemy has an island in the middle of that sea, and he is gleefully waiting for them to get stranded on it. Throw out the lifeline. Love them like family – because they are.

Follow the process, but focus on the product, and pray that God will make it something beautiful.

PRODIGAL PRAYER

God, help us. Help us to do the hard things for the right reason. Help us to follow the process, but to believe for the product. Help us to do everything you want us to do, even the things that seem counterintuitive and dangerous, but help us to do it all with a heart like Yours and with the full intention of following through to produce the beautiful result that You desire and designed.

And please, Lord, give us a heart for the hurting. Let us see what You see. Show us how to do what You would do. Let us change the spiritual trajectory in our families and in generations to come.

Lord, remind us to approach everything with a "there but for the grace of God go I" mindset. Whatever side of a situation we're on, may we not think more highly of ourselves than we ought. May we not hand Satan a victory, and may we build what matters in eternity.

Thank you for making everything beautiful in Your time.
In Jesus' Precious Name, Amen.

DAY 12

IT IS ENOUGH

"Sufficient to such a man is this punishment, which was inflicted of many. So that contrariwise ye ought rather to forgive him, and comfort him, lest perhaps such a one should be swallowed up with overmuch sorrow. Wherefore I beseech you that ye would confirm your love toward him."
– II Corinthians 2:6-8

Scripture Reading: II Corinthians 2:1-11

I am so, so grateful that God's endgame is always restored relationship. I am so glad that His intention is never a life-sentence of "lost" or an eternity away from Him.

As humans, we give up on other people almost daily. From the prodigals who walked out, to the people who annoy us, or don't think like us, or somehow disappoint us, we write people off constantly without a thought. Praise God, He doesn't treat us the way we often treat each other.

And while we may shut the door on other people, God is

knocking on those very same doors. My father used to say that if you have "breath in your body and sense in your head", God is still working on you.

As we discussed previously, the process outlined in Matthew 18 and lived out in I Corinthians 5 is a must, but if you believe that, then II Corinthians 2 is a must-read. Here, Paul encourages the Corinthians to "reaffirm" their love for a repentant prodigal. In other words, he tells them to go the extra mile in building up this man, to go out of their way to let him know that he is loved and forgiven. He talks about the possibility of this unnamed man being "swallowed up with sorrow" (Psalm 34:18, 51:17, Proverbs 17:22, Jeremiah 17:9, Romans 8:1, I John 1:9, 3:20).

There is so much wisdom in Paul's words. Our tendency is to hold a prodigal at arm's length until they prove themselves. But that's not the heart of God. Repentance trumps condemnation, and once broken, people need to be built back up (Romans 15:1, I Corinthians 9:22, II Corinthians 13:9, Ephesians 4:29-32).

The enemy will tell them that they'll never be truly forgiven, that people will always see them differently, always hold their past against them. As Christ's image-bearers, it is imperative that we prove the enemy wrong every chance we get. God brings the prodigals home, but once they return, He tasks us with doing everything we can to keep them there.

When I got right with the Lord in my mid-thirties, I was blessed to be surrounded by Christian women who loved on me, encouraged me, and built me back up (Ecclesiastes 4:9-12, James 3:14-18, Hebrews 12:12). They knew my sin, but they knew my repentance was real, and they helped me to move forward with a renewed sense of purpose. Had they not been the hands and feet of Jesus to me, I likely would have eventually gone back to my sin. Previously cloaked in shame, I had gone back before, but they reaffirmed me in faith and forgiveness, and the love of Christ compelled me to stay where I belonged.

I am grateful to this day for their willingness to invest in me, and I must encourage you to invest in the returned prodigals that dot your path (Hebrews 13:1, I John 2:10, Jude 1:22). Whether they came back last week or last year, the same sorrow that led to their repentance can lead them back to sin. Be the person who affirms that there is no more condemnation and no more sorrow needed.

Better yet, be the person that propels them into a life of purpose, allowing God to put His trademark Romans 8:28 spin on their prodigal period.

I'll say it again, what is under the blood stays under the blood, and what is left is white as snow. Treat it as such.

PRODIGAL PRAYER

Father God, I thank you for the people that you have used in my life to encourage me and build me up in my faith. Please allow me to be that person for someone else.

Whenever a repentant prodigal is in my path, show me how to reaffirm them in Your love. Prompt me to go out of my way to be Your hands and feet to them. Open my eyes to the ways you want to use them, so that I can affirm them in those specific areas. Help me to believe that You can and will make all things new. Let me see the possibilities in a broken life that is handed back to you.

Father, please don't allow us to be swallowed up in the sorrow of what You have forgiven. Help us all to forget what

is behind and to press on in Jesus's Name.
   Lord, prove the enemy wrong once again and let me be a part of it. You are able. Thank you for all You have done and all You are doing. Thank you for working through broken people like me.
   I love You, Lord. In Jesus' Name, Amen.

DAY 13

RESTORE SUCH A ONE

"Brethren, if a man be overtaken in a fault, ye which are spiritual, restore such an one in the spirit of meekness; considering thyself, lest thou also be tempted.
Bear ye one another's burdens, and so fulfil the law of Christ."
– Galatians 6:1-2

Scripture Reading: Galatians 6:1-10

I have a handy and infinitely creative husband, and so my house is filled with restored things. From pallet wood to leftover paneling to garage sale finds, he has taken what could have been trash and turned it into some of the most beautiful treasures in our humble home.

That right there is the heart of God – wooden vessels, lovingly and patiently restored until they hold as much spiritual value as their gold and silver counterparts. And maybe even more so, because their surprising beauty emboldens the ongoing restoration of more and more seemingly worthless vessels, elevating the value and usefulness of the whole collection (Romans 9:21, I Corinthians 1:26-29, II Timothy 2:19-21).

In Galatians 6:1-10, Paul exhorts the church about restoring the weak links and the wooden vessels. And when God's people choose to engage in this process, it can help to avoid some of the more painful processes we've discussed.

For nearly every prodigal, there is an opportunity to head them off at the pass. Most prodigals aren't born overnight, they are cultivated over time – a culmination of growing personal sin and growing corporate neglect.

Now don't misunderstand. Any prodigal is responsible for their own sin. They exercise free will and reap what they sow, but we as the church are constantly sowing, too, and many prodigals are the product of our refusal to bear one another's burdens. It's way too easy to roll in and out of church, and again, to check the boxes on our spiritual to-do lists, without ever engaging in the struggles of others (Micah 6:8, Luke 10:25-37, Romans 12:15, Galatians 5:13-14, I Thessalonians 5:14-15, James 1:27).

I guarantee you, there are potential prodigals under your nose right now. They need someone to speak up and bear their burden, not a prophet of doom, but someone who is willing to sow into their situation for God's great cause in their lives. They need loving intervention. They need to be engaged (Psalm 126:6, Matthew 5:13-16, James 5:16, Jude 1:23).

I'll admit, engagement can be messy. We each have our own problems, right? We have a million demands on our time, and we have our own homes and our own spiritual wellbeing to think about. All those things are true. But as members of the Household of Faith, we are tasked with maintaining that household – not just the building, not even just the ministries, but the individuals and their individual burdens.

Again, this takes a whole lot of prayer. It takes a willingness to get your hands dirty with other people's problems, a willingness to be robbed of time and depended on by people who aren't really yours to worry about. And yet, they are yours to worry about, because if your child, or spouse, or best friend were the one to be headed off at the pass, you would hope someone else would try to stop them from taking that road.

It takes an eye on yourself, to maintain your own spiritual integrity, put on the full armor of God almost hourly, and be certain that you are "spiritual" enough and humble enough to do the restoring (Romans 12:3, Ephesians 6:10-18, Philippians 1:9-10). It also takes an eye on others, to see the struggling, to note the signs that someone is weakening and starting to go under, to be ready to dive in before they really start to drown.

My advice to you – look for the deepest pockets in your church (and I'm not talking about money). Find the real spiritual strength-building opportunities, where people are diving deeper into God's Word, deeper into prayer, and deeper into self-sacrificing service than most of the stuff that clutters the church calendar. Those deep pockets will help you build the spiritual stamina to tackle a prodigal before they wander off.

We can't fix everything. We can't stop everyone from taking the road to destruction, but in my heart of hearts, I have no doubt that God calls us to try.

PRODIGAL PRAYER

Father God, open my eyes to see the potential prodigals who need engagement. Give me a heart to sow into the lives of others so that prodigals can be prevented from leaving in the first place.

Don't allow me to neglect their need or turn a blind eye to their struggles. Give me the compassion to help them now. Strengthen me spiritually, so I can help strengthen others.

God, I know You are a Restorer. I know You can bring beauty from ashes. But God, if You want me to bear someone's burden, if you can use me to prevent them from going down the prodigal road, please show me that. I want to engage. I want to be used by You. I want to restore what You want to restore as soon as possible.

Use me for Your purposes and Your glory. In Your Holy Name, Amen.

DAY 14

PETER THE PRODIGAL

"Simon Peter saith unto them, I go a fishing. They say unto him, We also go with thee. They went forth, and entered into a ship immediately; and that night they caught nothing.
But when the morning was now come, Jesus stood on the shore: but the disciples knew not that it was Jesus."
– John 21:3-4

Scripture Reading: John 21:1-19

Not all prodigals look the part. Peter had occasional moments of brilliance, even moments of bold faith, but then came his inevitable three-fold denial of Jesus. And Peter fell fast.

After some bitter weeping and a reunion with the other disciples, Peter is still struggling when we find him fishing in John 21. Laden with guilt, even the empty tomb wasn't enough to lift his spirits, and he probably both longed for and dreaded his next one-on-one conversation with Jesus.

Peter is suffering from a spiritual identity crisis, and weighed down by failure and uncertainty, he quietly goes back to the life he knew before his calling. There's no spectacular sin, no sordid trail of transgressions, just an anticlimactic loss of spiritual purpose and personal connection to Jesus.

He's back in his boat, fishing unsuccessfully once again, and probably wondering why he bothers.

I have sat in this prodigal seat, too, where failure feels final, and despite forgiveness, restored fellowship and renewed purpose feel out of reach (Psalm 51:10-13, I Kings 19:2-8, Isaiah 62:3-4, Jeremiah 20:9, Ezekiel 37:3-6). And I would wager there's more than one of those seats occupied in every Bible-believing church at any given time.

But Jesus is about to grant Peter a do-over.

Calling to them from the shore, Jesus tells the weary fishermen to cast their net on the other side, resulting in a déjà vu, net-breaking catch of fish (Luke 5:4-10). But Peter could care less about the fish. As soon as it dawns on him that Jesus is there, he is swimming frantically to the shore and to the Savior.

I love Peter's raw determination and desperation to get to Jesus. But notice, he started out just fishing. This passage shows us a man who figures he's slid all the way back to where he started. He can't bring himself to go to Jesus – until Jesus comes to him.

What follows is a good hot meal and a pivotal conversation that will propel Peter into a lifetime of ministry – ministry for which his very failures have prepared him.

I submit to you again that there are Peters sitting in our pews

– quiet prodigals who are waiting for someone to have a pivotal conversation with them, like Jesus would if He still walked this earth. These people have been uniquely designed for service by the Creator and Redeemer Who forgives all and wastes nothing (Jeremiah 18:3-6, John 9:4, Ephesians 2:10, Titus 2:14, 3:8). They are the disciples that you and I are supposed to be making (Acts 14:21-22, Ephesians 5:1-2, I Timothy 4:2). They are the ones that we are supposed to be provoking to good works. They may even be the ones who lead our own prodigals back home.

Can I tell you I have a running list in my head and my heart of restored prodigals? I pray for them regularly, encourage them every chance I get, and sometimes, I dream that they will be able to reach the prodigals in my family. I believe that God might use one of them to relate to my prodigals on a level that I never could. I don't know when God will work or how He will do His perfect will – but I believe.

And in the meantime, those trophies of grace are serving. Rather than simply lining a shelf, they have become vessels of honor, serving where others could not, making a difference and making disciples.

Not because of what they got right, but because of what they got wrong, and how Jesus made it right.

And that's true for all of us. Right?

PRODIGAL PRAYER

Father, show me the restored prodigals who need encouragement, love, and spiritual affirmation. Open my eyes to see what You want to do and who You desire to use, so that I can serve Your purposes.

Make me a blessing to those who are struggling to find their identity in You. Give me opportunities to pour into them. Remind me to pray for them, and please raise them up in tremendous ways to build Your kingdom, bring You glory, and bring other prodigals home.

Maybe they can even bring mine home. I know nothing is impossible for You, and I believe You are always working and You waste nothing.

Use me in spite of me. In Jesus' Name, Amen.

DAY 15

HOME SWEET HOME

"Ho, every one that thirsteth, come ye to the waters, and he that hath no money; come ye, buy, and eat; yea, come, buy wine and milk without money and without price. Wherefore do ye spend money for that which is not bread? and your labour for that which satisfieth not? hearken diligently unto me, and eat ye that which is good, and let your soul delight itself in fatness. Incline your ear, and come unto me: hear, and your soul shall live; and I will make an everlasting covenant with you, even the sure mercies of David."
– Isaiah 55:1-3

"Come unto me, all ye that labour and are heavy laden, and I will give you rest. Take my yoke upon you, and learn of me; for I am meek and lowly in heart: and ye shall find rest unto your souls."
– Matthew 11:28-29

Scripture Reading: Isaiah 54:1-14

Let's establish one thing. On the worst day, God is still good.

I tell my husband all the time that our worst day is better than most people's best day. And if you know Jesus as your

Savior and also have the benefit of living a first-world life in a free country, then I would wager the same is true for you (Psalm 68:19, 103:1-5, Nahum 1:7, James 1:17).

But when a prodigal steps away from the safety and shelter of home and church, one of the great temptations is for the folks back home to live in perpetual mourning for that tragedy (I Samuel 16:1). Believe me, I understand the unbearable pain that a prodigal departure can cause. I'm not trying to deny that. Prodigals leave holes in homes, churches, and hearts, and there is a time to mourn. But it is only for a season (Psalm 30:5, 40:2-3, Ecclesiastes 3:1-8, Daniel 2:20-22, Hebrews 11:6, I Peter 1:3-7).

If we have faith that God is working, using the pain and the process (along with His wealth of resources and creativity) to bring our prodigals to repentance and to bring them home, then we cannot mourn forever. There must come a point where we turn our eyes upon Jesus and realize that we are in the land of the living, He is our portion, and He is still good.

One of Satan's strategies is to use our own feelings of hopelessness against us and against our prodigals. When we allow ourselves to get stuck in the muck and mire of all that has happened and we can't get unstuck, we are handing a win to the enemy.

You need to remind yourself that God is still good – even when your prodigal is gone. Don't allow yourself to live under house arrest, in the midst of your prodigal's rebellion. Your Heavenly Father still loads your life with benefits on a daily basis. He has not forgotten to be gracious. His mercy is not gone forever (Psalm 77).

Don't let your prodigal see you living in unrelenting misery over their mistakes. Why would they want to come home to that? What does that tell them about your God? What kind of hope does that give them? Be honest about the pain they've caused but allow yourself to keep accepting good from the hand of God (Matthew 5:13-16).

I know you are weary, but Christ offers rest (Matthew 11:28-30). I know you carry a burden, but He wants to take that burden from you. Praying for prodigals is exhausting, but God blesses endurance and shows Himself strong on our behalf (II Chronicles 16:9a, Isaiah 40:30-31). And He promises rest, even when rest seems out of reach.

You don't need to heap guilt on them. God is working on that, and only for the purposes of bringing them to repentance (Job 13:15, Hebrews 12:6-7). Leave it to Him. Let Him do the work that only He can do.

And when you can carry on in Christ, continue to serve, continue to smile and praise God and enjoy the blessings of your inheritance, that sends a powerful message. It paints the beautiful picture of a sweet home, a softly glowing light on the porch, a slightly open door, and a hope worth revisiting.

PRODIGAL PRAYER

Jesus, You know the hurt in my heart. I thank You for caring, for being near to the brokenhearted, and for offering to take my burden. Help me to lay it at Your feet, Lord, and help me to keep going.

Forgive me for allowing my situation to blind me to Your blessings. You have been good to me. Everything I have is from You. Thank you for giving me another day to praise You, to serve You, and to hope in You.

FOUND: 21-DAY DEVOTIONAL

I love You, Lord, and I thank You for loving me. Please take this burden from me. I trust You, and I want to live in the center of Your will. In Your Name I pray, Amen.

DAY 16

RESTORATION BUSINESS

"Then Ananias answered, Lord, I have heard by many of this man, how much evil he hath done to thy saints at Jerusalem: And here he hath authority from the chief priests to bind all that call on thy name.

But the Lord said unto him, Go thy way: for he is a chosen vessel unto me, to bear my name before the Gentiles, and kings, and the children of Israel:For I will shew him how great things he must suffer for my name's sake.

And Ananias went his way, and entered into the house; and putting his hands on him said, Brother Saul, the Lord, even Jesus, that appeared unto thee in the way as thou camest, hath sent me, that thou mightest receive thy sight, and be filled with the Holy Ghost."
– Acts 9:13-17

Scripture Reading: Acts 9:1-17

I'll admit, some prodigals can be scary. There are the quiet ones (yes, my hand is raised, and yes, we need to be watched), the crazy ones (the ones who fear nothing and throw away everything) like the young son in Luke 15. And then there are the mean ones like Saul, fueled by offense and anger and blinding bitterness. They're a frightening bunch.

In Acts 9, Ananias is flat-out scared. God wants Him to go to Saul, and Ananias is not looking forward to it. Saul's reputation precedes him. He is the single greatest threat to the disciples of his day, a hunter and a hitman for the chief priest with written permission to wreak havoc in the lives of Christians. And Saul has been ruthless. Many have already suffered at his hands, and Ananias has no desire to be next.

But for all his misgivings, Ananias possesses one simple trait – obedience – and it takes him where common sense would not otherwise go. Obedience and faith are often synonymous (Joshua 24:24, I Samuel 15:22-23, Jeremiah 7:23, 42:6, Romans 4:3, Hebrews 11:8). In our flesh, we want to know how everything will work out ahead of time. We want assurances that we're not going to be wronged or used or taken advantage of, but God doesn't always give those guarantees in the restoration business. If He did, what would we need faith for?

You may be called upon to restore the prodigals that scare you the most (Psalm 27:1, Isaiah 41:10). The ones that will really challenge your faith, your patience, and your fears.

Here's what you need to know – God is in the business of using restored prodigals – even the scariest ones. Especially the scariest ones (Ezekiel 36:26, John 4:27-29, I Timothy 1:15-16). When the Holy Spirit woos a soul back to the Lord, it is always for a two-fold purpose. The first purpose is the reconciling of that soul to God for the glory of God, the second purpose is the reconciling of others through the testimony of that former prodigal (also for the glory of God). And some of the angriest prodigals make for the most amazing testimonies.

That was the only assurance Ananias got. God had plans for Saul. The rest was not his to know, but I think God knew that Ananias would come around, in spite of His fears. Hopefully, He would say the same of you and me.

Are you ready to get into the restoration business? There's not much to know, and really, there's nothing to fear. You simply need to obey.

PRODIGAL PRAYER

Father, I know You have not given us a spirit of fear. Help me to be a part of Your restoration business, and help me to have a spirit of power, love, and a sound mind.
I know that You never ask me to go anywhere without You, and You will give me everything I need to help those that You want me to serve.
Please help me to be strong and to have courage. Help me to do what You want me to do and go where You want me to go – for Your glory. In Jesus' Holy Name.

DAY 17

BETTING WITH BARNABAS

"And when Saul was come to Jerusalem, he assayed to join himself to the disciples: but they were all afraid of him, and believed not that he was a disciple. But Barnabas took him, and brought him to the apostles, and declared unto them how he had seen the Lord in the way, and that he had spoken to him, and how he had preached boldly at Damascus in the name of Jesus."
– Acts 9:26-27

Scripture Reading: Acts 7:54-8:4

It's a crazy thing. We pray for miracles, never actually expecting them to happen. We beg God to turn things around, and then turn all skeptical when He does.

In Acts 9, Saul is ministry-ready, but the ministry isn't ready for him. Before leaving Damascus in a basket lowered from the city walls, Saul astonished the believers there with his newfound faith and his on-point preaching. But the disciples in Jerusalem aren't so easily convinced. After all, they live in the city where Jesus was crucified and where Saul was commissioned by the high priest to continue the slaughter.

Understandably, Saul's one-eighty is a hard sell, but then along comes Barnabas – the "son of encouragement." Barnabas bets on Saul, or more to the point, he bets on the life-changing power of Jesus Christ. Facing down the skeptical disciples in Jerusalem, Barnabas vouches for Saul and uses his own credibility to confirm Saul's calling (Acts 4:33-37, 9:26-27).

The results still reverberate through the church today. The Apostle Paul (as he would become known) would establish churches through multiple missionary journeys, would write 13 books of the Bible (II Peter 3:15-16), and would die a martyr at the hands of the Roman emperor Nero (II Timothy 4:6-8). Countless souls would be saved along the way and countless more have since been saved as a result of his writings. Not bad for a questionably restored prodigal.

But back to Barnabas. In those early days, would Saul have made it without him? The two would have their differences (Barnabas invested in more than one prodigal, and it took Paul a while to appreciate that), but Barnabas accompanied Paul on his first missionary journey and changed the course of Christendom (Acts 15:25-26).

Ask yourself, who needs you to be their Barnabas? I submit to you that every restored prodigal needs at least one, and none of us can have too many (Numbers 6:24-26, Psalm 3:2-4, 66:16-20, 115:11-13, Proverbs 12:25, 25:11, Colossians 4:5-6, Philippians 1:12-14, II John 1:4).

Those who have fallen, fled, and fought God need someone to see their potential while they are still "a great way off." Shame, guilt, and the doubts of others are all tools that Satan can use, but God calls us to "lift up the hands which hang down" (Hebrews 12:11-13).

It's hard to believe in your own change, if no one else can see it (II Corinthians 5:17-19). And especially when old temptations inevitably come knocking on the door, any prodigal would be vulnerable without a Barnabas in their corner.

Be the Barnabas, the encouraging, prayer-fueled optimist who runs to meet the returning prodigal where they are. They may not be perfect, but neither are you. They may need some cleaning up, but you did once, too (Ephesians 5:18, I John 3:17-19).

Believe in the life-changing power of Jesus. Bet everything you have on it. God blesses that kind of faith. God gives that kind of mercy. Give and it shall be given unto you.

PRODIGAL PRAYER

Dear Lord, please use me in the lives of restored prodigals. Let me be the Barnabas that encourages them and helps them to believe in what You can do in them and through them. Help me to see past what they have done to see what they could be in You. Let me have a part in Your work of restoration and reconciliation.

Give me the courage to stand up for restored prodigals, to vouch for them, and to trust that You are faithful, regardless of the outcome. No matter what others may do, I want to do what pleases You.

Bring the prodigals home and show me how to meet them where they are. Give me sincere compassion for Your trophies of grace. In Jesus' Name, Amen.

DAY 18

DEEP-END DISASTERS

"And some days after Paul said unto Barnabas, Let us go again and visit our brethren in every city where we have preached the word of the Lord, and see how they do. And Barnabas determined to take with them John, whose surname was Mark. But Paul thought not good to take him with them, who departed from them from Pamphylia, and went not with them to the work.

And the contention was so sharp between them, that they departed asunder one from the other: and so Barnabas took Mark, and sailed unto Cyprus; And Paul chose Silas, and departed, being recommended by the brethren unto the grace of God."
– Acts 15:36-40

Scripture Reading: I Timothy 4:11-16

In Acts 12:12, we are introduced to young John Mark. He is mentioned, not because of what he was doing, but because of what his mother was doing. Mary, the sister of Barnabas, was hosting a church in her home and holding an all-night prayer meeting on behalf of Peter. And while they're praying, an angel is walking Peter out of Herod's prison and dropping him off on Mary's doorstep (Acts 12:1-17).

By the end of the chapter, Mary's son, John Mark, is leaving on his first missions trip with his Uncle Barnabas and the Apostle Paul (Acts 12:25). And by the chapter after that, he has left them, prematurely heading home and utterly failing to complete the mission (Acts 13:13).

John Mark is a ministry kid and (with Uncle Barnabas as a father figure) one of the early church's first P.K.'s (Preacher's Kids), if you will. He has been thrown into the deep end of ministry, and he has ended up a deep-end disaster. While planning their next departure, Paul and Barnabas will have a less-than-Christian parting of the ways, and John Mark will be their point of contention (Acts 15:35-40).

John Mark's journey resonates with me in a big way. I am a pastor's daughter with a past and as such, I have a special burden for the high-risk ranks of kids raised in the ministry.

To be a P.K. or a missionary or ministry kid of any kind - where one or both of your parents are called and serving actively and you are automatically commissioned by extension – is a peril all its own. You look the part. You hopefully act the part, and therefore, you are simply given the part without question.

My three siblings and I lived in a loving Christian home, but we were casualties of ministry life. We traveled for years and then settled into a small country church. We were loved and always treated like family by that sweet congregation, but during our critical teen years, there was very little there to encourage our personal spiritual growth and nothing to keep us in check (Deuteronomy 6, Proverbs 22:6, 29:15, Ecclesiastes 12:1, I Chronicles 22:5-6, I Timothy 4:11-12).

We were always part of the ministry team – singing, teaching younger kids, working at events and in the nursery – but we were rarely ministered to. Everyone assumed we were okay, and we were not. We were spiritually adrift – in church, but not growing, serving constantly, but only by default. We were present, but not invested. And aside from our exhausted, overcommitted parents, no one was actively investing in us. It was another deep-end disaster.

By God's grace, John Mark would turn around later in life. His Uncle Barnabas would continue to take him under wing, (in spite of his failure) and the investment would pay off.

John Mark would be a leader in the church at Jerusalem, would write the Gospel of Mark (Peter's account of the life and ministry of Jesus), and even Paul would eventually team up with him again, testifying that John Mark was "profitable…for ministry" (Colossians 4:10, II Timothy 4:11, Philemon 1:24, I Peter 5:13).

But here is my plea. Church, rally around your ministry kids. Pray a hedge around them. Build real relationships with them and counsel them. Check on them. Don't assume that they are as spiritually strong as their parents. Rather, assume that they have a spiritual target on their back and protect them from the fiery darts of the wicked one.

Most importantly, make sure they are growing as much as they are serving and give them a place to grow (Deuteronomy 6, Proverbs 1:8, 22:6, 23:26, 29:15, Isaiah 54:13, Ecclesiastes 12:1, I Chronicles 22:5-6, I Timothy 1:1-12, 4:11-12, Hebrews 13:16-18).

The greatest gift you can give your pastors, missionaries, and leaders is to invest in their kids the way that they invest in you. And by God's grace, the road to destruction will be a little less traveled, and we will all reap the rewards.

The prodigals of today can be the preachers and teachers of tomorrow.

Believe it.

PRODIGAL PRAYER

Lord, thank you so much for the godly pastors, teachers, and leaders who have invested in me and my family. I thank you for their prayers on my behalf.

Father, please protect their families. Please work in the hearts and lives of their children. Keep them close to You. Don't allow them to have a shallow relationship with You. Let them really know You and love You and serve You with a whole heart.

Don't let the enemy discourage them or lead them away. Use them for Your glory.

And Lord, show me how I can be a blessing to them. If I can encourage a ministry kid in their walk with You, please don't let me miss that opportunity. Make me a blessing to the ministry families in my life and make those kids the preachers and teachers of tomorrow.

Thank you for making them a blessing to me. Use me to make a difference in their lives. In Jesus' Name and for Your glory, Amen.

DAY 19

PEOPLE IN THE PATH

"If thou count me therefore a partner, receive him as myself. If he hath wronged thee, or oweth thee ought, put that on mine account; I Paul have written it with mine own hand, I will repay it: albeit I do not say to thee how thou owest unto me even thine own self besides." –
Philemon v.17-19

"My little children, these things write I unto you, that ye sin not. And if any man sin, we have an advocate with the Father, Jesus Christ the righteous: And he is the propitiation for our sins: and not for ours only, but also for the sins of the whole world."
– I John 2:1-2

Scripture Reading: Philemon

More recommendation than exhortation, the single chapter Book of Philemon is a plea on behalf of a reformed prodigal by the name of Onesimus.

By this time, Paul has a full grasp of his own prodigal story (I Corinthians 15:10, I Timothy 1:15-16), and he has seen

John Mark (referenced here as "Marcus", v.24) evolve from prodigal to profitable for ministry.

And while in prison, Paul has a not-so-coincidental meeting with a runaway slave. And here's the not-so-coincidental part. Paul knows this slave's owner. The slave in question, Onesimus, belongs to Philemon, whose house also serves as home to the Colossian Church (Philemon 1:1-2). Onesimus had a Christian master and a back row seat in the church, but it took imprisonment with Paul to make Jesus Lord of his life.

Paul leads Onesimus to Christ and then becomes his advocate, writing Philemon a recommendation letter for the slave he already owns. But Paul knows that Onesimus is not the same slave who ran away. He is changed, and Paul is willing to bet his own reputation on it (Philemon 1:16). He even offers to pay out of his own pocket any debt that Onesimus might owe Philemon (Philemon 1:18-19).

What a beautiful picture of our Savior, Who paid the debt He did not owe. Paul embraces his role as a Christ-like advocate placed directly and deliberately in the path of this prodigal (Romans 5:6, II Corinthians 5:21, I Timothy 2:5-6, I John 2:1).

My friend, God is constantly orchestrating the placement of people in our paths (Psalm 37:23, 51:12-13, Proverbs 16:9, Isaiah 30:21, Mark 16:15, Luke 14:23). Sometimes we are placed to help them. Sometimes they are placed to help us. Sometimes both. Paul would acknowledge that Onesimus had been a blessing to him, as the rebel's road became a two-way street of service (Colossians 4:9, Philemon 1:10-14).

That scenario is still possible today. God put people in my path to lead me back to Him, and I am so grateful He did.

Not one was coincidence. Each one was conviction, compassion, and confirmation from a loving God.

Pray for those people in your prodigal's path. It could be someone they work with, a neighbor, a friend of a friend, a radio program, YouTube video, or even a total stranger. There's no limit to who or what God can use in your prodigal's life.

And look for people in your path. You may not know it, but every day, you are surrounded by prodigals that are on other people's prayer list. Make it a two-way street. Give and it shall be given unto you. Pray on, walk on, and pay attention to the people in the path.

PRODIGAL PRAYER

Dear Lord, I believe that You are working in my prodigal's life even now. Please put just the right people in their path at just the right time to help them find their way back to You. Prepare their heart even now to respond to the messenger that You have chosen.

I know You are sovereign over all things, and I believe You can lead them to people who love You and can represent You well. Bless those people for their willingness to be a light to my prodigal.

Please help me to represent You well, too. Allow me to be the Christ-follower who leads someone else's prodigal back to You. Fill me with understanding and compassion. Fill me with Your Spirit.

May You have Your way in every situation, and may I care about other people's prodigals as much as my own. Show me a need that I can meet and help me to meet it for Your glory. Use me, Lord. In Jesus' Name, Amen.

DAY 20

FOR A SEASON

"For perhaps he therefore departed for a season, that thou shouldest receive him for ever; Not now as a servant, but above a servant, a brother beloved, specially to me, but how much more unto thee, both in the flesh, and in the Lord."
– Philemon v.15-16

"Blessed is the man that walketh not in the counsel of the ungodly, nor standeth in the way of sinners, nor sitteth in the seat of the scornful. But his delight is in the law of the Lord; and in his law doth he meditate day and night. And he shall be like a tree planted by the rivers of water, that bringeth forth his fruit in his season; his leaf also shall not wither; and whatsoever he doeth shall prosper."
– Psalm 1:1-3

Scripture Reading: Ecclesiastes 3:1-11

Seasons come and seasons go, and that's a blessing, because it assures us that even the hardest seasons will have an end. And when you're praying for a prodigal, this is a scriptural truth that you need to keep close (Deuteronomy 3:3, Psalm 30:5, John 14:3, Galatians 6:9, Revelation 20:5).

Paul points to the value of a season in his plea to Philemon, a godly man who got a raw deal from a runaway slave. Please note, slavery was as much an evil in Bible culture as it is today, but Christianity turned (and still should turn) the concept of social classes on its head, as all people, bond or free, were equal before Christ (Galatians 3:28, Colossians 3:11, 4:9, Philemon 1:16, I Peter 2:17-19). Combine that new reality with the fact that Paul testifies to the kindness and character of Philemon, while Onesimus lands himself in prison even after a successful escape from Philemon's household, and we can assume that Onesimus left a good home in a bad way.

But Paul points to a season – a time that has a definitive beginning, but an equally-definitive end. And Paul puts a Romans 8:28 purpose (after all, Paul wrote Romans 8:28) on that season.

That's a hope you can hang your hat on. Your prodigal may be gone for now, but it may be what everyone needs, and most especially, what your prodigal needs. In the story of the prodigal son (or sons), both brothers lived through the same season, but one lived at home in status quo, while the younger brother got the reality check of his life – far away from home. In the end, the housebound brother was bitter, and the homeward-bound brother was better – forever changed, in fact.

As you pray for your prodigal, ask God to help you endure whatever season is necessary to plant the seeds for eternal, soul-saving change (II Chronicles 30:9, Psalm 90:16, 100:5, 102:28). Don't hold on to them so tightly that you keep them housebound, perhaps even hell-bound, and marinading in their own bitterness. Fight your flesh and the instincts that urge you to take control of this situation (Job 23:10, Proverbs

3:5-6, I Corinthians 13:4-8, Hebrews 12:11, II Peter 3:9).

It is not yours to control. It is yours to release. Give your prodigal to God, let them take that journey, walk that road of failure, consequence, and hard times. Let them know you love them, but let them go, and trust that God has sovereignly designed a definitive end to this difficult season.

Better yet, believe that God can bring about a better season. In Psalm 1, a season of fruitfulness and flourishing is described, far away from the counsel of the ungodly, the way of sinners, and the seat of the scornful. By God's grace, that season can be yours. It can be the prayer-paved road that brings your prodigal home (Psalm 91, 124, Isaiah 61:3-4, Jeremiah 29:13, 32:40, Luke 15:20-24).

I believe that someday, we will meet Philemon and Onesimus in heaven, and they'll seem much more like brothers than anything else. And as they tell you how they came to be so close, I imagine that both will testify that a certain season paved the road for a new beginning.

PRODIGAL PRAYER

God, I release my prodigal to You. I trust that You will use even the most difficult season to work out Your eternal purposes. You can work it all together for good. You want all people to be saved. You are a Deliverer, and a Restorer. You are a Master Planner. Your plans, timing, and ways are perfect, and You alone control the times and seasons.

Take control of this season, Lord. Help me to stand back when I should, be still when I should, and trust that You are working all things together. Forgive me for the times that I try to control things on my own. Forgive me for holding on too tightly to the situation and not tightly enough to You. Make my heart sensitive to Your leading and don't let me do anything that works against what You are doing.

I love my prodigal, but I know that You love them even more than I do, and You know what's best. Have Your way. In Jesus' Name, Amen.

DAY 21

PRAY ON, PRAYER WARRIOR

"Although the fig tree shall not blossom, neither shall fruit be in the vines; the labour of the olive shall fail, and the fields shall yield no meat; the flock shall be cut off from the fold, and there shall be no herd in the stalls: Yet I will rejoice in the Lord, I will joy in the God of my salvation. The Lord God is my strength, and he will make my feet like hinds' feet, and he will make me to walk upon mine high places."
– Habakkuk 3:17-19

Scripture Reading: Habakkuk 3

In Habakkuk 3, the prophet has not gotten the answer he wanted. Instead, he receives the very news he dreaded. No immediate relief. No redemption on the horizon. In fact, the enemy is advancing, and the horizon is the backdrop for an impending invasion.

God will redeem His prodigal people one day – but not yet. And in the meantime, the worst of the world will have its way with them – until God says it's enough.

If you are still there, watching the world have its way with your prodigal, you are not alone. In fact, dear reader, I am right there with you – even as I write this book. But this is where the rubber meets the road. This is where you have to dig in, pray harder, pray more often, and just plain pray.

It's what you can't see that matters (II Kings 6:16-17, Psalm 115:3, Ephesians 6:12). There is a battle behind the battle, and your prayers ensure that you are invested in the right side. God is lining up events and people and opportunities. Satan thinks they're his doing, but He doesn't know what God is doing. Hold on to that hope.

If faith is the substance of things hoped for, then increasing our faith means living a hope-soaked life. Our enemy wants to fix our eyes on every last sign of impending doom and certain failure (I Peter 5:7-9). But we know better. We are blood-bought children of the King, and we've seen what grace can do (Psalm 13:6, 66:16, 111:4, Micah 7:18-19).

Barren fields and empty stalls (the Old Testament equivalent of wasted years and an empty seat at the table) won't deter us. Weeping may last for the night, but the same God Who made that night lifts the sun above the horizon to signal a new day, new mercies, new morning (Psalm 35:27, Lamentations 3:18-26, John 16:33).

Pray on, Prayer Warrior. Pray like you can already see the sun peeking over the hills. Pray like you remember a million mercies. Pray like you've seen miracles before, and you fully expect to see them again (Psalm 23:6, Jeremiah 29:11, Malachi 3:16, Romans 8:31-39, I Corinthians 2:9, Ephesians 3:19-21).

The Father is listening. The cloud of witnesses is sitting on the edge of their seats. The angels are just waiting on the Savior's signal, and all of heaven is rooting for your prodigal's return.

Don't give up now.

PRODIGAL PRAYER

Father God, I praise You today for all You have done in my life, for all that you're doing right now, and for all that You're going to do.

Lord, although my prayers haven't all been answered yet, even though I can't see exactly what You're doing, even though I don't know how long I'll have to pray these prayers...

Although _____,

Although _____,

Although _____,

Although _____,

Although _____,

Yet I will rejoice in You, Lord. I will joy in the God of my salvation. You are my strength. You are working, and You are good. Thank you for delighting in mercy. Be merciful to me, a sinner, and be merciful to my prodigal. I trust You, Lord, I praise You, and as long as I have breath in my body and sense in my head, I will pray on. You are worthy of my prayers and my praise. In Jesus' Precious Name, Amen.

MY PRODIGAL PRAYER LIST

MY OWN PRAYER NEEDS

THINGS GOD HAS TAUGHT ME

ANSWERED PRAYERS & PRAISES

ANSWERED PRAYERS & PRAISES

ANSWERED PRAYERS & PRAISES

ABOUT THE AUTHOR

A pastor's daughter with a past, Greta Brokaw is the author of three volumes of **Heart Medicine Devotions for Women**.

In addition to writing devotions, Greta is a Christian singer and songwriter with two CD's, **Heart Medicine Music** and **God's Not Done**. She has been singing in churches for well over 40 years. Like her books, her music is a collection of scriptural, grace-filled songs meant to encourage hearts and point them to Jesus.

Greta is available to speak at your next women's event or to sing at any church event.

For additional booking information, books or CD's, email gretamay24@gmail.com or visit myheartmedicine.com.

Made in the USA
Columbia, SC
31 October 2024